Warsi,

Thank you so much for your time and energy in reading & reviewing my work!

— Frank

WILD SOIL

FRANK R. CHAPPELL

Copyright © 2016.

All rights reserved. No part of this book may be reproduced, stored, or transmitted by any means—whether auditory, graphic, mechanical, or electronic—without written permission of both publisher and author, except in the case of brief excerpts used in critical articles and reviews. Unauthorized reproduction of any part of this work is illegal and is punishable by law.

All photography is the property of the author. All engravings are the property of Woitek Skop, and have been published with the express permission of the artist. For more information on the artist, please write to the following or visit him on Facebook:
23 Rue de la Garenne
17420 St. Palais sur Mer
France

Interior Graphics/Art Credit: Frank R. Chappell and Woitek Skop

Library of Congress Control Number: 2016918668

ISBN: 978-1-4834-6116-8 (sc)
ISBN: 978-1-4834-6115-1 (e)

Library of Congress Control Number: 2016918668

Because of the dynamic nature of the Internet, any web addresses or links contained in this book may have changed since publication and may no longer be valid. The views expressed in this work are solely those of the author and do not necessarily reflect the views of the publisher, and the publisher hereby disclaims any responsibility for them.

Any people depicted in stock imagery provided by Thinkstock are models, and such images are being used for illustrative purposes only. Certain stock imagery © Thinkstock.

Lulu Publishing Services rev. date: 11/10/2016

No, it is impossible; it is impossible to convey the life-sensation of any given epoch of one's existence—that which makes its truth, its meaning—its subtle and penetrating essence. It is impossible. We live, as we dream—alone.
-Joseph Conrad, ***Heart of Darkness***

To the God and His messenger who whispered your name in your mother's ear as she slept, and to you, Anna-Maria

Contents

Foreword xiii
Preface xvii

An Adolescent Revolt 1
Youth 3
A Natural Cure 4
Digestion 5
The Suppression of Instincts 7
Concerns on the Last Day of April 8
NYOT 9
Third 11
To my Father, on a Father's Day in Madison 12
Missed the Train 13
A Portrait of Freedom 14
A Portrait of a Trailer Park Mother 15
A Portrait of Loneliness 16
A Portrait of a True Man 17
A Portrait of My Ancestors 18
Nephew's Third Birthday 20
Common Thoughts Conveying Culture Naturally 21
Processing & Lamenting 22
The Crucifixion 23

Nameless Prayers 25
1 27
2 28
3 29
4 30
5 32
6 33

7	34
8	35
9	36
10	38
11	39
12	40

The Product of Ritual 41
   Homes of the Gods 43
   Morning Meditation 44
   Monks and Monkeys 45
   Death of a Believer 46
   An Argument of Faith at Station V. 47
   HET 48
   The Resurrection of the Dead and the Life of the World to
      Come 49
   Religio 50
   I Sing the Lament of the Golden Calf Builders 51
   We Are Almost Finished Here 53
   Images of Death 54
   A Monastic Deliberation 56
   Saint Melancholy 57
   In the Hollows of the Earth 58
   No More Worries 60
   Sunlight From a Slit in the Blinds 61
   Final Judgment 62

Devotions 65
To Anna 67
   I 68
   II 70
   III 71
   IV 72

V 73
VI 75
VII 76
VIII 77
IX 78
X 79
XI 80
XII 81
XIII 82
XIV 83
XV 84
XVI 85

The Invigoration 87
   It begins as Affect 89
   Natural Religion 90
   All At Once 91
   The Ones Who Fear God 92
   A Thoughtful Trance 93
   A Blank Mind is Worthless 94
   Thoughts on Solitude 95
   Worldbody 96
   A Beatitude 97
   Cynics 98
   Perfection in Imperfection 99

Meditations 101
   Autumn 103
   He Worshipped Trees 104
   Peaceful Love 105
   Reality is Socially-Sanctioned Fantasy 106
   A Sharp Pill 107
   Where the Devil Hides 108

Rock Bottom 109
The Uncertain Beast 110
Pyrrhic Victories 111
The End Result of a failed Marriage that began with such
　　burning Love 113
Ancient Struggle 114
Roaring Chickens 115
Country Settlements 117
Social Logic 119
Blood of the World 120

Foreword

The traditional social contract permits a person to uphold a conviction about faith or the ultimate purposes of life, but the same person ought not to despair about love or destiny. The conventional cultural script enjoins a soul to be tethered to various bodies in a grid of security; but the same person ought not to languish in the sorrows of loneliness. Typical aesthetics grants that a human heart may find delight in natural wonders and in the odd turns of the human form; but then the same senses ought not to suffer revulsion nor compulsive attraction to the same. Apparently, nobody told Chappell that you could not have it both ways

But Frank Chappell does each of these operations (that is, each one and its opposite) in the confines of a single day, or even, apparently, single minute. Reading his poetry gives one the impression of hiking along the intersection of tectonic plates: diverse landscapes and microclimates clash. One skins one's knee on an unexpected rock escarpment, and his ears and lips turned blue amid the frostbitten pastures of his soul. Alternatively, a spa of sensual consolations opens up with warm invitation, and soon Frank has anointed and massaged you with words spilling out like an unction.

The background of this author like in the foreground of his poetry, is strikingly disparate. Born and raised in the ethnic enclaves of a mining village in the rural valleys of Southwest Pennsylvania, his education in a local college was a vehicle he rode into a global engagement with life. He has traveled abroad again and again, studying non-human primates in Central America, paleoanthropology in Africa, pilgrims in Mexico, Buddhist monkhood in Southeast Asia, and Balinese ritual in Indonesia; where incidentally he first met the French woman would become his wife. He served his time in the Air Force Reserve, attended graduate school in Illinois, and returned to his home, employed in the drama of assisting at-risk youth in a group home.

Back in Pennsylvania, he passionately observes the generations which preceded him, laid waste by mills and mines, yet filled with the poignancy of family bonds and the bondage; religious devotion and superstition. He participates in the theater of the generation which will follow him, often overwhelmed by their wounds, sorrows, addictions and darkness; yet just as much amazed at the exuberance of life itself coursing through them. Frank Chappell's poetry moves like a pendulum from paradox to contradiction, and back again. Perhaps, every now and again the pendulum crosses some invisible medial line, and Frank sees and writes about what the world sees and considers all the time, some balanced, moderate and middle place, where things make sense. Chappell gets it. But he is not buying it.

The poetry you are about to read is not derivative of the experiences that the author suffers or enjoys. Let the reader be aware that Frank Chappell, who lives with varying intensities at work among youth, working with his hands like his father on land and building, and engaging his friends and family in all the follies and joys of life, is most alive in the secret act of generating a poem. But the words he puts on paper are not the shadows of the things he experiences so much as they are the raw experiences themselves. Such is what he knows how to make words to do, as do few others. And if you love someone, you would do well to give them such an adrenaline shock of life as literature like this.

Mark F.X. Gruber M.Div., PhD.

Preface

I don't ever remember reading a poem before I actually wrote one. I was twelve. I had just gotten off the telephone with a girl who I had some pre-pubescent crush on who was older than me and I jotted down some ridiculous, dramatic attempt to translate what I now understand to be jealous longing into a piece called "Tears." I think I lost that one—most likely in a pile of Playboys in my teens—but I recall the first lines reading, "tears for a friend, I have none/ these are for a best friend," or some garbage like that.

I hate myself now for even having remembered that. How embarrassing, right? Besides, no one wants to hear someone's quasi-nostalgic-first-poem memory spelled out for them like it was some nocturnal emission they were dying to have again let alone read poetry anymore. I don't often think poetry is dead, I know it is. There are too many sentimental saps waiting to be filled with some dainty simpleton's holiday card-style trash, too many pages filled with memorial reflections of bygone emotional outpourings, and too many deeply disturbing one-liner-zen-attempts with obscure references masquerading as intellectualism for it not to be on its last breath, and yet, here you hold this compilation.

I am no poet. I am simply someone who has the privilege to be able to feel and describe some interconnectedness with my own vicissitudes, a universal human experience, and perhaps a small portion of insight, and now, wishes to toss it into the air of societal judgment. While I am sincerely grateful for any patronage that pays me enough to reach my break-even point on the expenses of this small, printed piece of myself, and do hope that what a reader finds herein both represents their experience and elucidates some portion of their lived reality in an original manner that generates insight, I have written this material ultimately for myself. I expect little and am greatly satisfied if I learn that these bits of thought enrich another's life.

I suppose I retract my previous statement—I'm allowed to do that—poetry may not be dead, but it is in dire need of revitalization, development, and promotion among amateurs. I have never forced myself to write, and to write professionally would kill me; I have no PhD in any subject let alone poetry. But, when I am moved occasionally, I know that I am conveying a piece of undiscovered humanity and performing a creative labor for myself that would make Marx proud.

I always believed that Literature is generative of consciousness; literature is consciousness-creating. That is, when we explore the interior domains of another's lived reality combined with both their interpretation of it and projection of meaning onto it, we have gained invaluable insight into a condition of life we had theretofore never considered. In compiling the experience of the *other* into one's own milieu, we find that we have enriched our perspective and can more fully appreciate a person, event, or situation with information we, in our limited experience, would not have otherwise been able to glean.

If what has been written here is inaccessible, I apologize; there are too many writers striving to condescend to a reader/seeker with labyrinthine or exorbitantly abstract diction and style, but a bit of a search for meaning is profitable for the soul. Poetry to me has always been a tool for sublimation: to process emotions and experiences into a dream-like heuristic device and produce some truth sans the constraints of proper grammar, punctuation, or even complete thought. The impressions of our sub-conscious and analytical thought of our conscious minds must be able to churn visceral and cognitive thought into a complex whole for a human life to be fully experienced. Poetry is this. It is the reflection of our individual agency vying with cultural expectations; it is our meaning machine spinning to create a cosmology wherein the sacred and profane coexist and intermingle; it is the preservation of philosophy and philology; and it is the entrance into shamanic trance in a "civilized" western societal context.

Having explained my own philosophical anthropology on the subject, a short preface of my work is appropriate here I imagine. The sections in this small volume are comprised of several years' worth of selected material from various stages in my psycho-social and emotional development that I felt could be shared in order for others of like-mind to extract something useful. If I am wrong, it wouldn't be the first time.

Some of them reflect the development of human experience as it corresponds to the spiritual journey undertaken from uncertain youth to uncertain adulthood in a developed, secular society. The human endeavor has always been imbued with the search for the Sacred; even in this postmodern era of secularization, of overly advertised atheism, of fanatical fundamentalism in both science and religion, superstition, new age trends, and consumerist fads reigning as new gods, we seek to make our lives meaningful and leave a lasting legacy. This impulse to care for what exists whether or not we do transcends belief and non-belief. Whether one believes that the ability of mankind to interact with a divine realm is a reflection of the existence of God and the soul; a social creation of the collective consciousness arising from the fact that we are aware of our own deaths and choose to deny them cross-culturally; or that the existence of religion and spirituality are merely a byproduct of an evolved brain, one cannot deny the monumental impact the realm of the divine has upon past and present human thought and behavior.

Other portions of this book explore the interconnectedness of Being we are capable of experiencing, rejection of all religious tenets, and complete nihilism: all facets of my own existence in particular and the human experience in general. Moving from adolescence, prayerful experimentation and reasoning, seeking results from ritual attendance and observing organized religion, growing in religiosity and finding even secular objects of worship, feeling enlivened by spiritual and intellectual work, and contemplating one's existential place in the both the Sacred and Profane are all present in the pages of this work.

If I have been anything throughout these pages, I have been refined in crudeness, complex in simplicity, and doubtful in faith. I have not chosen, but instead often feel utterly compelled to bear witness to a way of perceiving reality that reflects simultaneously an appreciation for a lifelong journey of contemplation and abhorrence for the same. I am privileged for this perspective, and sincerely hope it has meaning to the extent that it may instruct or guide others to begin a course of genuine introspection. Any journey without anthropological contemplation is merely a conglomeration of ritual acts in a vacuum and serious study of oneself is necessary for a life well lived. True growth occurs when you are open, aware, and able to relinquish some control to the wilderness of the first Socratic Principle: recognizing that wisdom begins with the admission that you do not know.

An Adolescent Revolt

Youth

remember
what it was like
when you wanted
me to be
laying under
your bed on
warm August mornings
waiting for your
parents to pass below
and avoid
getting caught
because you had
caught me
the night before
in you

A Natural Cure

Depression clings on the back of hypochondria
you don't need to kill yourself,
you're already bleeding out of your skull.
anxiety is death itself.

Only small deaths can save me now.
that release that comes from
ridding oneself of
the weight that creates

the only pleasure left
that touches the reptilian core
where the primal rage resonates in its cell
where the primal rage resonates in its cell

Digestion

I am
feeding myself the
mythos of the culture
masticating the lies of
our generation
digesting the facts and data
licking research from my molars
savoring the taste of the demographics

I doubt
all that was said
as I swallow the placebo of
complacency I required to accept
we belong
to the degree to which
we follow
we belong
to the degree to which we agree

I have
drawn a full Cartesian Circle
with the bones I found between
the muscles I am now relaxing

I am
and I can feel the sour pills cling
to the walls of my stomach
as they pass
a catharsis in my gut
that I have passed

And you
cannot share
in my syntheses

The Suppression of Instincts

I watched her at the alter
Mass unfolding
winding down like
a dying calf, wounded
wet with slow death

And her hair folded softly
over a taut, white cheek
and deep, black eyes gazed past
the veil of flower sacrifices
to the soon-to-be Risen Christ

I noticed her lower lip creased
under the upper: two levels of Being
(Heaven touching Earth) accompanied
by a small, elongated nose
complimenting every ray of light
streaming from the stained glass behind her:
as if she were a Virgin

Concerns on the Last Day of April

I have always desired to create a work of art
to paint emotion, and make people feel
through gazing at green grasses swaying in
breezes by blue waters and bleached foam
that gently froths near clean, white houses

or to capture black agony and crimson anguish,
but I cannot draw, and I cannot paint,
and I cannot contain in any work
those pieces of broken etcetera items
that invade my awareness

it frustrates me that I am restless,
but I can feel sometimes
between those days when I am dissatisfied,
when I have touched that essence,
that I have found something that allows me
to better appreciate that flowering crab tree,
a lingering figure guarding venetian blinds,
spreading wide, red blossoms
and I wonder often of my death
and when it is that I am to be released
and the mind I have sculpted
is to be effaced

NYOT

Our dawn breaks at 2 a.m. now
lights and birds and creaking floorboards
don't kill the daddy longlegs
crawling on the library floor
it's good for something

Silence is eloquence
but songs carry you home
unwanted sleep consumes us
in the hours devoted to unusual revelry
We are gods unto ourselves

I faint
what cruelty that I could not spend
another hour devoted to the upkeep
of that flame you follow home

We wake, and sit to soak
sun on hot deck boards
and read Playboy and poetry
how indicative of our characters
we believe

my anthropology is
affected by our belonging
budding Epicureans
we feel

and for the first time,
I was exactly where I wanted to be
when we donated the money left over
from the strippers to the church
laughing, laughing

Third

my hair is never in order
continually disheveled and
chaotic—like the
battlefields my grandfathers
tread—dodging mines like sleeping bears
and lead flying through boat hulls
limbs and pieces of mangled flesh
rotting into the foot-churned soil

the ways of the old have vanished,
but my father keeps his hair
neat and clean,
accurate and correct

To my Father, on a Father's Day in Madison

I will try, but not my damnedest,
to remain in this peace with you and savor it.
memories of my mother
I have inflated, romanticized, and altogether recreated
to add benevolence fill me now as well.

I intellectualize your deaths
to find a catharsis
that begins where pain ends.
parental idioms form the basis of our
conceptions of God: Mother Mary, God the Father.

Line by line I plant
like the rows of pines we tried to grow,
myself for you always,
but like them,
few take root and soon decay.

You are pine, maple, oak, birch, and chestnut.
you are me and I am you
and we are tangled in roots that only recently
ceased choking the life from each other
and I fear it is too late.

Missed the Train

George talked to me today
George wanted to talk I think
About his life and past

George wanted to work on the railroad
Be strong like his father who worked late
But he got his teaching degree to avoid hard labor

George said to me, "we watched the lights come
down the tracks in the dark. Trucking has
replaced the railroad."

My father drives a truck

A Portrait of Freedom

A flash of gray shot against
    reflected light from the falling snow
    there beside me.
He had slid easily from curb to road
    one thin wheel behind the other
    soaked in water and white with chipping paint
I am looking through
    the wall of flakes falling steadily
    there at him
His hair sprouts, gnarled, tangled, long, and greased
    from lack of a roof and effort to stay clean
    his jacket is as tattered and thin as his face
    the cold would have destroyed that
    family of lucky lice without his beard
I have heard tales of Buddhist monks
    walking through the rain
    without getting wet

He is holy—separate, unhindered
    by that capitalist net—
    he gave up so long ago
Franklins fall from his pocket
    and alienation from his yellowed, gritty teeth
    as he throws his head back and laughs
    at the thought
    of becoming
    dead.

A Portrait of a Trailer Park Mother

potential wasted in a trailer park
the next cure for cancer dies poor
smoking after being
smoked out of a life
as a little girl
young and crying in a high chair
for smoking mommy two feet away
but so much farther

i cringe to think of the tears wasted
over hidden toys in the infinite couch
on which you sat wasting teen years
with cigarettes and weed

while your daughter, wasted,
brings home another man,
and waking the next day, feels
a sense of self in wading through
saturated prophylactics and touches
her belly praying she did not bring
another disease into the world.

A Portrait of Loneliness

It is night
empty
my apartment.

but I cannot escape the sound
even in sleep
of rustling vertical blinds
like some stranger waiting

paranoia sets in
like strange shoes in mud
they carry weight

Loneliness is 10,000 muddied shoes
Bostonians most likely
there is an air of class to him
after all

so I reach behind vertical blinds
and pull him right out
by his collar as he shrieks!

and we laugh
over some cake and drinks
at the thought of what
he previously had in mind for me.

A Portrait of a True Man

Lions have adapted to hunting in water now
I hear from the old safari leader with scorched skin
and deep earth-filled scars dug across
his wrinkled face like trenches of war
capped with an Antarctic beard and Apartheid brow

He hasn't worn shoes in what? ten years?
and his feet are incredibly calloused
like an elephant or bovid or some new cloven species
pounding dust into dusts' dust
impenetrable

I can't help but wonder though
about those defenseless springbok
and wildebeest and zebra near shallow pools
soaking their proboscises in warm,
sun-heated chemical

He is a lion
and cannot stand the sight of
such beautiful flesh without his scent upon it
it is easy to take what is not given
with only a little justification

A Portrait of My Ancestors

I.
My grandfather
taught me how to die
better than any ancestor.

His shallow breaths reverberated
joy and pleasure
until the end.

His final words to me,
I lived a good life, and a joke,
were couched in a laugh.

II.
Dreams are the gods of savages, truly.
He comes to me now at night
in his brilliant white uniform
and his taut, bronzed skin shimmering with youth
beside my aged, smiling grandmother
and welcomes me home.
What are you doing here?
It is not me, he says,
and I wake; even the civilized react.

III.
Now I give him
flowers and candles
prayers and Masses.

And he visits me often in death
to remind me, unintentionally of course,
of my ingratitude.

I breathe memories
and they flee like little white dogs
down depressed streets
and young men boarding ships to war.

Nephew's Third Birthday

"What is 'die' Uncle?"

(he has no sense of the verb tense yet
and I didn't want to explain "to die")

"That's when you don't live anymore."

(i searched for the most simplistic answer
not wishing to delve into
the theological possibility of an afterlife)

"I don't want to die, Uncle."

(he used it correctly now, without thinking
grammar programming itself naturally!)

"Me neither."

(i can offer as much comfort and solace to him
concerning death
as i could to a cancer patient who,
upon speaking the same thing,
exhales and
slips away)

Common Thoughts Conveying Culture Naturally

so much more ink has been wasted
in idleness and boredom than
in the pursuit of truth

youth should be spent in leisure and learning
and middle age in work and family
with old age in leisure and teaching

black hooves overturn brown earth like a plow
horse and man are as natural as man and woman;
i saddle them both with affection and distrust

poetry is the literature of experience
it operates with religion already built in
the anthropologist should turn to poetry as culture

Processing & Lamenting

The day's redundancies arrive and
depart with annoying regularity
anticipated and suffered with
monotonous usualness

Extraordinary phobias and passions
wax and wane without regard or
concern though they could have lit
a fuse of events to magnificence

Ignored antisocial and interesting
misanthropic tendencies are buried
among the slothful tombs of
cultural norms maintained by drones

Outlandishness is celebrated as
liberalism, but true anomie is stifled
and labeled as psychoses;
it must be the individual, they say.

The Crucifixion

I sat adamantly,

    my back firmly against the
    wood of the pew,
    the grains pressing into vertebrae.

And I was hoisted at their mourning.

    I reassured myself,
    struggling against faith,
    that there is scanty evidence of this man at all.

Nameless Prayers

1

the air outside in this
cold, Pennsylvania winter
is tinged with the smell
of burning wood
not over-powering enough to choke
but just enough to taste
like incense at Christmas Mass
wafting gently through the ether,
bodies, and souls of the faithful
the air is incense over a God-filled land

2

just stop thinking
and let the bricks rise out
of the ground—
great walls of our immigrant ancestors—
and box you in and
make you sublimate the
panic into some
worthwhile boredom
before you pack it up and hop
out onto the rails on that
Last Journey
where all of your baggage
gets left exactly where
the metal grinds your bones
into the same shale
that so many foreign pickaxes
once landed upon
building that bright future
you hate

3

these people
are so reluctant
to put their Christmas decorations
away

cheap nativity scenes
on church lawns lit
in freezing January weather
ten degrees. Jesus.

God is not the
luminescent electric hum
emanating from Joseph's
worn and painted face

he had a dream once
of Mary and took her
as his wife
even dreams prompt action in reality

4

i had been talking of old times
and laughing as though
i were an incontinent old man

i cannot believe the age
i have gathered about me
in such a short year

april snows in Pittsburgh

i haven't the slightest clue
where i'm going as though
i were a cloudy-brained fish with a 6-second memory

reset, reset, reset

i realize i cannot memorize everything
and keep it to sound intelligent as though
i were a professor of some archaic science

but i can still appreciate the light invading my window
i can't stop pushing every complaint onto everyone around me
as if i were reliant on so many for satisfaction

addictive co-dependent relationships

i'd rather be alone at times
as though i were a hermit in a cave
with a head full of yellowed teeth

and tales of my flights into the collective consciousness
or of how i saw the Earth from above
a coffin of my own

5

bandage me
wounded to the bone
and my heart sinks

doubt is what is left when
you've run out of options
or just can't think of any new ones

maybe we should kill
what we love
before it brings us pain

bandage this gash
in my cultured self
so that i may bleed from somewhere else

6

some kid
some ignorant bastard
took his thin finger and
his long arm
lowered it into
the aquarium and pinned the
brightest goldfish
into the gravel
pinned it!
his finger is like
a nail through the side
of a golden wall
the Western Wall,
ruined, has faced this
but look how quickly
the fish's body
turns black
and passes so quietly
into upside down death

7

love moves itself, shifts and mutates
what cruelty, right?
to have such a bright box filled
with light and wonder turn to stone and wood

but stone can be heated and
wood reinforces
strong iron nails secure one to the other
and it becomes equal again

that bright box has turned from
Romeo-death-breeding-suicide-desire-filled sentiment
to an appreciative permanence
solid and sustaining

forgive my heart
when this box of stone
turns cold
it is constant and unbreakable

8

in a wall of 1,000 skulls
    what distinguishes
    yours
    from the rest?

Nothing.

it is the flesh
    that carries
    the mark
    of the test.

9

a mist forms
in the creeping morning
over the creek below this elevated camp
and the heat of the fires still scorch
empty faces and full heads near it

i dreamed of two women
woven as one vindictive lover spiting me
Christ, save me from such horrors!

writing in darkness is not arduous work
pen and ink flow just as easily as
water, blood
through pre-designated courses

i write in the dark
and pray for mist to envelope me
and fires to singe me
and for nightmares to burn like paper in Hell

we make ghosts of each other in life
and efface memories we once relied upon
for nourishment

logs slip now deeper into flame
and illuminate parchment like
the desk of some scribe
all thoughts are ancient when they derive from experience

in this purgatory we wait
melancholy lifts slowly like mist over a creek
and fire, gladly, burns away a life made in haste
with lovers now departed

10

a man that sleeps every night
has no passion

seeds sprout amidst stones

but there is a happiness in unproductiveness
it is a much different joy than
slothful malaise

one must first be productive
and choose to rest with the former

the latter is a disease

11

lines move
and intersect

and millions of skin particles shed
and coat the floor like unseen snow

from this biological imperative
all is new again

and everything goes away

12

i cannot live
with things undone
anymore

walls unpainted
tiles not laid
trim not nailed in place

i cannot think
with projects left
unfinished

friendships unsalvaged
deaths unmourned
guilt unattended

i attack like
like all must be done now
because i cannot bear to think
of what i have neglected to do

The Product of Ritual

Homes of the Gods

I enjoy the tap of my shoes on concrete
it resembles the sandstone of Angkor
such a shame
a temporary kingdom at war with the wind
will inevitably lose

I have a new habit:
visiting the homes of gods
and placing myself in the past

churches and temples are time machines
architecture, symbols, rituals
preserve a place in time
and insert it here, now

I am moving into the
homes of the gods
because I can't freeload on
your couch anymore
I am enamored by daily activities
dishes, laundry, eating, yawning
all smeared with the oil of
predictability and beauty
holy in itself!
we are the gods whose homes
we envision in our trances
our ideals are bricks
baking in the sun
and our actions pour the mortar
we pray and stack, pray and stack

Morning Meditation

I watched three birds
sitting on a power line
waiting for the morning sun
to rise over the hills
and dispel the morning mists
that hung around the veranda
in the early blue of a sky
waking from a bestial slumber

Man is a moral animal: fretful and malignant.

I do not understand at times
the logic underlying virtue
but that its attainment is
desirable along with finding purpose and etcetera

The morning fades much too quickly

Monks and Monkeys

These Buddhist monks chant in the night
and make the land a paradise
and the lake, the cosmic ocean
but they are simply sitting under trees
singing like our arboreal ancestors
must have done for mates

Now, we envision ourselves much differently
    we are the image of God.
    we are the product of Will.
    we are imbued with a soul.

Do these songs of monks reach across
the span of space, ever-expanding,
and reach some foundational Cause in the dark?
after all, we are star-material
and the blood in our veins, seawater

Who is to judge
whether we sit in denial and delusion
when we are the products
the perpetuation
and creation of such wonderful
chemistry?

Death of a Believer

A fly came into the church
and flew around the priest's hair
it tossed about in sparse strands
of coarse black
oil coated
reed-like structures.

The candle near the pulpit,
luminescent and warm,
attracted the paper wings of the fly
and it settled down on the wick,
and was consumed by the fire.

The air around the candle moved only slightly
and the hair of the priest was not disturbed
as he sermonized
about money needed for repairs.

An Argument of
Faith at Station V.

It was an awkward situation:
a conflict of insecurities

Simon raged at me, stared
and bored a hole through me
from his throne-like position
above my head, on the wall
I could tell from his cold, wooden gaze.

His forest green cap tamed brown and
terra cotta curls—carved features—and
the tip of his hard nasal structure pointed
like a spear at me, with eyes that met mine.

Where is your conviction? he burned
Where is your reason? I shouldn't have said

His biceps flexed as he gripped the cross
a viper with sunken fangs in cold, dead flesh
I looked away, he gazed harder now
tension built and sweat
drenched my forehead
I looked back
and found his composure frustrating
he knew he was forced into faith.

HET

I am bound now
St. Sebastian with arrows
in arms and legs

Am I the martyr with righteous blood
of some cellophane reality?
hold it to the light and relish in its pink hues

They should have given him a quick death
but prolonging the suffering racked up
a few more graces on the heavenly board of gold stars

Confession always gave me those golden graces
keeping track of sins, remembering prayers, and entering
dark closets where demons hid as they were exorcised

The Resurrection of the Dead and the Life of the World to Come

The mind is a social creation
consciousness is cultivated
formed by figures whose impact
has yet to be quantified
memories are the creators of personhood

I spend time in Hell
and bask in privations
I have made a home of my memories there: a retreat
this simple hut design has grown into
a Victorian with trap doors and secret libraries
leading to shrines for the worship
of any period's icons

Anastasis
I am always standing up
after I kill myself
In my house, no one dies

Religio

white plastic covered furniture
in a roped off living room
gets sullied by the boots of the worker
trespassing onto unknown snow-covered soil

this is the system under which
we were born
uniting us
generations

macabre images of my salvation
still visit me
and you better believe
that it predisposed us all to seek
liberty and release

change the myths to something less severe
a Socratic gentleness for the children
to ease their transition from desire to reason
and I will not pretend anymore
that my mother was an immaculate virgin

I Sing the Lament of the Golden Calf Builders

I have been on many mountains
but never saw God
though the scenery at the summit
was quite breath-taking and He was
probably standing right next to me.

Lucky you, Moses, for your unwanted privilege
of looking into a shrub and finding
the Divine looking back at you!

I sing the lament of the golden calf builders
we are too hasty, too frivolous, too impatient,
too needy, too lustful, too whatever.

I sing the lament of the golden calf builders
whose faithfulness and desire for purity
have been quenched with flesh and drunkenness.

I sing the lament of the golden calf builders
whose God-given logic took from them
the ability to see reason in the irrational
Christ, why didn't you just Herod a sign?

I sing the lament of the golden calf builders
because I cannot wait for a man to walk
down the mountain, and I cannot wait for
righteousness to arrive from a blazing cloud.

I pour into the mold with golden hands
because I cannot wait
and I weep bitterly for my sin.

We Are Almost Finished Here

The heavy black circles
attest to the indignant worry of youth
not any type of long-night-long-day
dragging-ass-tired schedule of work

I've only been immersing myself
again and again and again in the sopping
bucket of my culture to remind myself
of some stable identity I once held

The Ivory soap and burnt candle wick smell
of my childhood inflames my olfaction at
odd times of the day, forcing me to recognize
a fleeting religious conviction, now gone

I am in the inner sanctuary
I am pulling at the curtain of the Footstool
I am wrestling with the angel
what hope can I have to gain in secularity?
Shall we lament the loss of grand illusions
and wish for the days when modernity
was not such a creeping grandmother
poisoning the well with her deconstruction?

Images of Death

Bones in the ground
I can't cry out as loud as the
words of the note you laid
under the rock on my tombstone

I'd come back and address
so many of your questions,
reprimands, concerns, and even
provide some witty commentary—
poking with invisible digits,
hollow and vaporous—
as you kneel before dimly-lit shrines
green candles encircle the blue Woman
crowned with white orchids

So many Catholic school days
spent standing on creaking wooden floors
filled with black nails
purple missal in hand
rosary beads too

What a concept: loneliness in the afterlife!
you'd think it would be stocked with
effervescent life forms sailing on clouds
and in between aurora borealis-like realms

What red and green and yellow gases
escape to carry souls
on their transits between stars
to God and you
kneeling in wonder still waiting for answers?

A Monastic Deliberation

Subordination is Freedom:
such iconographic images entering
the mind—saltatory conductions fusing
ideals with reality in a syncretic mix of
reciprocal, undulating, warring, symbiotic
mental constructs—what taxonomic hermeneutic
is worthy of explaining such paradox?

I'll be damned if I give into
tempting notions of ball-and-chain contentment!
to have nothing is to gain everything
a counter-cultural finger to the hellish state of
American materialism. What am I doing?
to whatever ridiculous muse, fates, or destiny,
I'll be right back, and peel away layers
of self-inquiry to reach some enlightenment
or nihilistic purgatory.

Saint Melancholy

Blank minds require company
and idle hands need work
behind closed doors we exhibit
our desperate selves
and bemoan our solitude

With others, we yearn to flee
Alone, we pray for kindred
there is no peace for
the capable mind surrounded by dullards
but hearts break for inferiors all the same

Brains fester like open wounds
stomachs clench with
adrenaline to digest
sleep becomes a foreign concept
blood runs like paint on
humid cellar walls
we hope to learn from this?

What brave souls are those
who accept their fates!
what courage exists
in the man who
stares into the face of Hell,
tastes its darkness, and
carries on with his plan!
surely, God admires the bravery
of the self-killing soul

In the Hollows of the Earth

No sensible man would insist that those things are as I have described them, but I think it is fitting for a man to risk the belief for the risk is a noble one...
                                        -Plato, *Phaedo (114d)*

In the hollows of the Earth,
our heads don't touch the surface
and the mist encloses the facades
that we place around the corporeal body.

It is where the four rivers flow
toward the Acherusian lake
I can find my faith
it lays there dead and cold;
the head of Nike.

In the hollows of the Earth,
where our ancestors emerged
and butted heads like golden rams
on the plains of some barren continent

We sat around camp fires
tired from the hunt
and gazed star-ward
and synapses fired, fired, fired
myths assumed a human shape.

Day broke in the hollows and the mist receded.
our skyscrapers broke into the ether
invaded the waters
and placed a blanket over the gold and green.

The temples in the air
where men spoke
to the gods that resided in them
have fallen.

No More Worries

drove past a cemetery
headstones in headlights
caught my father's attention
not much catches his attention
but "there," he said,
"is where you have no more worries in the world"
and his dry hands cracked
on the steering wheel as
a freezing wind killed
the remaining blades of green grass

Sunlight From a Slit in the Blinds

I have a sin of fear, that when I have spun/ My last thread, I shall perish on the shore;/ But swear by thyself, that at my death thy Son/ Shall shine as he shines now, and heretofore;/ And, having done that, though has done,/ I fear no more.
         -John Donne, *A Hymn to God the Father*

I.
Sunlight from a slit in the blinds pouring over a bed
a blessing to the observer
thank God I could notice it
and be rejuvenated

II.
Laid down and felt the warmth
spilling over my face
a private bath in luminescence

III.
Opened my eyes to divinity
and it stared right back
disappointed that I closed myself
and gripped my stomach in pain

Final Judgment

I am a blue demon
and you laugh at me
because I have this
silly hue about me,
but weep with me now
because I have forgotten:

    the sun
    the touch of a woman
    the touch of a man
    my father
    my mother

    (yes, I was human)

    sweet breezes
    and silky sands

Autumn aromas have given way
to eternal winter
and I shovel in
forkfuls of the damned
who have also forgotten:

    the Sun.

Do not become me.

Devotions

To Anna

I

I watched two farmers
walk in a field of
high green.

Their hands caressed
each stalk of nameless vegetation
with such expectation.

I know expectation
ruins relationships
but you don't.

You refuse, and rage against it.
Thank you for that, for
you are one of the few remaining strings
of kindness holding me
to Humanity.

Suddenly, we are these two,
walking in this vast
Eden of Green.

And we touch all living
with the caress of hope
for their success, and
sorrow for their deaths.

The secret of these moments
reveals itself in
Experience.

And we touch that as well
and play like children
without a thought of sin.

We are already aged
in experience, and the
lines on our faces are
reminders and journals
of laughter and tears.

Bury me here
in this
Green Memory!

Reality is torture now
and I cannot bear the idea that
I must wait until
another harvest to taste
these fruits that we have
so carefully planted.

I will walk with you still
though we are ghosts
to each other.

We yearn for flesh
in an Eden
of Memory.

II

I am a phantom
walking listlessly about
stalking other shadows
down endless, dimly-lit halls.

I am a figment of your imagination.
I do not exist in the same reality as you,
but we move together somehow.

It is strange to think that you exist at all
beyond my touch.
I feel you still;
your shallow breaths
heave and fall like the lungs of a sleeping lioness.

You exist in me, and I, in you.
even if you were not real,
I would not wish to live
without you.

III

Snow falls like so many screaming moments
of time without you, but in utter silence
I count time now, not in seconds or minutes,
(*chronos* time)
but in moments of clarity with you
(*chirus* time)

I repeat it to you, "like I said, like I said"
close the screens and lay down in bed
and you invade me still
in impressions of an altered life
I have never dreamed of changing course
so much in one lifetime

I compile now, shards and shreds,
parcels and pieces, words and memories,
and sew them together—these things of
you and I—and create our culture
and stare out windows at blanketing snow
and oceans, cold and treacherous

Distance is not measured in time and space anymore,
but in memories sewn and expectations planted
even now I have you in your absence
a mental structure before me
unable to surpass its counterpart in reality
I will not forget that you have chosen me,
and I will make a life worthy of you.

IV

nothing is worth doing without you
the smallest endeavor requires the most energy
my sweat, I fantasize,
is the ocean between us
and I navigate it to you
closer and closer
I glide and swim and sail to you
my work will set us free
and if you wait,
I will scoop you up
in the grit and the sand and tides
and bring you home

V

I have forged through rainforests,
temples, caves, and mountains.
I have seen sunrises from rock ledges,
sunsets from beaches with waves
taller than the green hills of my home,
and smelled the fires of poverty
burning in the same night air
where monks chant.

Now, I follow you
and trapse in your footsteps.
I have crawled on my knees to sacredness,
hidden in places of sheer wonder,
but never with so much devotion as
I have in crawling to you.

You are my madonna now,
and I throw myself at your feet.
I no longer seek wisdom
for its own sake, but only insofar
as it can be used to please you.

Forgive me if I gird my heart in steel
and armor in your presence,
for if I did not,
your gaze would rip it to tatters.

I am strong
because I am weak for you.
I rampage, break my fists,
and pound my chest in the sun while
in the dark, I wrap you in me,
and like a child,
I sleep.

VI

It is not these twilight hours
that throw me into tempestuous moods,
but you.

You give me your essence and I covet more.
your death is not enough—
I understand that now—not enough.

Seconds are hours, hours are days.
I become less and waste away
to increase for you.

My body is broken, aches, and cringes
like a mutilated, scourged Christ;
I have never prayed to die before, until now.

What do we do with this?
I drag my corpse to you
and feign to stand stalwart.

I am in you, and you in me, no,
I am you and you are me, and I beg you
to keep me in the present when I stray into the past.

My eyes are heavy and I fall into stormy sleep
relieved, for a short time, that I can escape us.
If God were merciful, I would never wake.

VII

I used to enclose myself
strong, fortress-like,
stoic in my demeanor
my conscience was a pane of glass:
deeds raining on smooth coldness, unrepentant

Now, something seeps slowly
to the surface, and I am not
a breathing callous anymore

I consider my pane
my words, my actions
have brought me to you
though this is not flattering
we gave up to preserve our shields

There are three solar revolutions to account for:
ages unto themselves
we emerge from gamete-soaked selves mending damage
and grow quickly into maturity

I have rescued you
you have rescued me
I am new and you are new
and we exist now
in the place of broken panes

VIII

I am not like this she says
I am this way because of you she says
my sweet, loyal girl,
marriage does not change us, we change each other
the negation of transformation is a fool's wisdom!

We are growing and moving
apart in body, together in mind
leaves follow the sun through slits in white blinds
eager and hungry to satiate unspoken desire
just as I follow, seek, and desire you

Few have been naïve enough to claim you
like laying claim to salty ocean breezes
skimming across sand-pelted skin!
you have belonged to no one; you are mine
and I breathe you in to keep me alive

IX

I lay awake in darkness
and dream with open eyes; I can almost see you
on beaches of white sand
without me.

Your body, frame, and self all point to
transparent water where you bathe.
I close my eyes.
where are you?

I create you in my mind when you are gone.
you are not this shape, but close it.
my misunderstanding of you
gives rise to so much frustration.

Every day is Hell without you.
so much stronger are my descents into darkness;
there is no prayer to lift me
from this mercurial state.

I beg for sleep and it laughs.
I die slowly without you.
and you, like some distant dream,
fade with the dawn.

X

we did not belong to each other then
as we do now

now, I kiss your feet in worship
and blaspheme with you

I am healed by Her water and
become one with us again

your saga tortures me at times
and I am desperate for you to efface our memories

remember what I said to you,
toes curled up, sitting,

"no matter what happens, I love you"
even on filth in a pagan land

XI

I have no skill except leaving.
at times, all that matters
is your ability to depart comfort
and seek new, wild soils.

I have become too comfortable
and conventionality does not suit me
without you,
the animal appears again.

I must shrug off
this coat of normalcy, and
kill the beast once again
with you.

XII

There is no rest with you
and your green eyes flash
with storms and squalls
on uncharted oceans churning
with the dead, swollen bodies
of attempted conquistadors
unsuccessful Perseuses before the Medusa
countless in number, shameful in their efforts

There is no taming what is wild
except in destroying wildness
eliminate the animal desire
by eliminating the animal
there, you have it
there is always a mare to be broken
before she throws you

XIII

I am good at loving you
at a distance
and when we are between seas

Boxes containing assemblages
of objects and artifacts
are actually me

I come to you in pieces
just like at the beginning
except now in material forms

Take these effigies of me
and know
that I give you what small soul I have untouched by cynicism

XIV

what architect constructed
the gentle convolutions of her ankle?
deep scarred skin flows like
a thousand streams pouring into
turns abounding over deeply buried
bone and sinew

we take our flaws and ball them up
like scratch paper we had written
all the wrong answers on
and swallow them down together
with our morning vitamins
we do well to challenge bruised egos with a taste of
disappointment and imperfection
it makes us real

hanging out in dumps and slums
frees us from the weight
of aesthetics and perfection-seeking
there is liberation in filth

XV

When I was young, I was free
and dangerous and rogue
then you tied me
in sweet and sacred
Servitude

I offer you tears in bowls
to drink like morning tea
joyfully, though upon offering,
it is a torrent of pain
but, you purge me

I am cleansed in cruelty
and bathed in your rage
I understand pain
and trudge through it wailing
to you, Redeemer

XVI

The everyday is no severe stone
milling away
when you wake connected
to land, to plans, to her

You go through Hell with me
and suffer through my flames
deserving none and taking all
your singed wings smolder and hide

You open me, and my chest cracks
and steams for healing
but such incisions are slow to dry
and instead, remain drenched

You drag me to evolve
because I cannot do it alone
your tears water stones in me
and make brooks on fertile ground

You are the fragrance I imbibe
and the life enlivening me
I have no other recourse
I have no other respite

I lose sight of your benevolence
amidst the harangue of these days
when I grind my teeth at night
I hold you away from me
I am terrified of my vulnerability
it breathes because you breathe
and when we traverse worlds
I forget the present

I will climb my own wall
to join you in a place
where we both laugh
and exist only for the others' good

I will take this gift
smothering in me
into the light of day
for it to flourish

The struggles we create fade
like sunsets over darkening paths
hover beside me always
when it is darkest between us

The Invigoration

It Begins as Affect

Sunday rolls around much too quickly
concentrating on the soft murmur
of a mother reading to her children behind me
tension leaves my back and
the hair on my neck pricks up
from chills
like years ago when my mother
sang to me as I fell asleep
on our soft couch in front of the Christmas tree
aglow with religion
small flickering lights
warm and inviting

Natural Religion

Jesus Christ,
the grass seems so green
after a few hours of rain
spring up brightly and without pain

and I feel so comfortable
like a meditation
like an out-of-body, out-of-mind
experience

I cannot deny the soothing effect
that faith engages in me
whispering down my spine
lyrics of archetypical falsities

and I can feel the shiver,
a conflict of smells more or less
as I pick apart memories and grow old
and sad thinking of when this must end

All At Once

I walk through empty and quiet rooms every day
in the same house
and gain new perspectives
the unfolding of memories and experiences
are like reading 1,000 books all at once

Emotions trail me like ghosts and gently footsteps
there is only sorrow when solitude is mourned
looking in mirrors reveals my age
in windows, my melancholy

I have often wished to see God stare back
from the shimmering snow and bare trees
there is only wind sweeping through woods
deafening, I am sure, to creatures therein,
but completely silent here above

It is a rare occasion when music can move me
and provoke some mood, but when it does,
I am unable to pull myself
from the depths it sinks me

Millions of lives have ended before mine began
and no one cares
I allow the thought to move through me
and possess my steps and learn from lives unknown
and mourn strangers I will join soon

The Ones Who Fear God

I am becoming weaker with age
not physically—like knees-cracking,
bones-rubbing, cartilage-disappearing
while I listen to the radio at 3:00 a.m.
type of weaker—another kind.

I weep, sob, and am completely destroyed
by the slightest sign of beauty.
just mention maternal care,
or a loving god,
and I need a new face.

I am arrogant, proud, and cocky,
but that ego flies screaming now.
it even wants to light candles
and join the ones who fear God
to mend my disfigured humanity.

I am no fundamentalist,
but I am filled with awe for
the ones who face demons, fail, and continue;
even this thought has already
brought me crumbling down.

A Thoughtful Trance

I am parked again.
It's cold.
Not see-my-breath-in-the-car-cold
but cold enough.

I am watching clouds pass.
They gain speed on the windshield
in front of me:
blurs of blues and grays.

They are in the windshield now
running over a hill of glass
like so many ghosts in battle
warring.

They say mystics find
the interconnectedness of all things
or do they simply unite universal symbols
in a comforting patchwork to purchase?
The feeling is here though.
Retreat glass-captured souls,
and rush into oblivion!
I will blink
and sent them all away.

A Blank Mind is Worthless

Bleak autumn nights
and softly illumined embers
still shimmering in moonlight and
the last true heat of a blaze
have finally ceased to be beautiful
and those dark, ashy coals
and rotted leaf reeking asphalt lanes
have become my death.

Inspiration flies with swift wings
many-winged, many-eyed,
it hides its face and soars
before any potential of a dawn
to ensure endless night.

No flaming sword guards these gates
and God departs
while angels remain
to pity this empty temple.

Thoughts on Solitude

I am growing accustomed
to silence again
and falling asleep alone.

There is no one here to anticipate
my waking
or make this place a home.

I watched the rain in the darkness
and saw some truth
and rolled beads and ropes to bargain.

I know I am not meant to last
and my death
will come soon.

I am not beaten
by physical ails
but pressure on the brain.
It is enough to make one sit
in the darkness and stare
at the heavy bullet on the nightstand.

When I am gone,
keep the silence, and this house
I will be the rain.

WORLDBODY

I know of other patches of shoe-trodden earth
exist beyond these cloistered windows
(the world, or whatever)

>But I have Greece on my tiled floor,
>Rome in the arches of my thresholds,
>Asia bustles in my pantry, and
>all of Africa in the sod burnt
>by the sun near the corner of that old,
>dilapidated well
>a desert oasis in the Kalahari
>beyond the front, paint-peeling porch

And I have no desire
to leave a world
that I am already in.

A Beatitude

My favorite time of the night
is just before I fall asleep
when the orange street lights send their glow
into my window and onto the wall, a sky.

I stare into the dark sky over
a sea holding an African sunset
impala skulls and Zulu spears in the darkness
and the refrigerator hums a mantra
and whisks me back to starry nights
with silence broken, no, not broken,
blessed by monks chanting and smelling of incense
it wafts in the air like the souls that
linger to be fed at Pchum Ben

I breathe deeply and taste their sweat
and African air and the electricity of
the appliances' light upon the slow, thick
atmosphere so dense and dark and still now
I dream before I sleep
Blessed is he whose dreams are memories.

Cynics

Diogenes watched a mouse from his
Rejection-smeared, skin-laden
Jug of wretchedness
And felt clarity and truth

Its needle-nose seeking crumbs among
Feces, twitching with seizures of pleasure
Upon finding some morsel of
Sustenance for the hour

I can only think of plague
And bitterness at its condition
And my only pleasure derives from
Maiming and smashing their grey visages

Is there any brain in the world
That does not impose order
And make meaning form the
Filth of existence

Perfection in Imperfection

Few absolute Evils:
there's always a hand reaching
from the depths into the
Light.

When you've paid your debt
in blood and consequences,
guilt and failure,
Rest.

You will never stop reconciling
or seeking repentance
when the system is
stacked against you.

Prepare to repair
and burn in the fires
of purgation
stage to stage and back again.
We make no progress
and do what we wish
not to do
reach and mourn, reach and mourn,
and celebrate your reaching.

Meditations

Autumn

There is no philosophy
to be applied to the soil from which
tall poplars protrude like shafts
of veined appendages to support the sea above.

There is nothing
to be added to the mosaic of green-turning-yellow
leaves scattering like gold paper:
detritus in a week!

There are no thoughts
necessary to attach to the silence
of empty forests,
for they are the origin of all thought.

There are no bodies
that do not burst and decay
in soil, leaves, and detritus
in the silence of empty graves.

He Worshipped Trees

There is some mysticism left
in tall, golden trees
sprouting in the grey
of bleak October mornings

Primate sensibilities awaken
and search for beasts and souls
within bark
and roots

There is nothing like a deep wood
to bring forth
crisp senses in
an awe-filled man

And make him consider is course
and the trajectory of his life
in terms of dense foliage and
the mysteries projected in sacred forests
I would gladly lay down
next to an ancient, hard-skinned giant
and seep into liquid as I stare into canopies
to feed these monsters

Peaceful Love

Peaceful love is foreign to me
there is a sophisticated violence to love
fierce are its tactics
complex are its stratagems
heavy and solid, its armor

It waits in shadows and depths
prowling and skulking like
rotten legionaries grinning and snarling
with black-rooted teeth
jutting, pearlescent, opal even,
from ancient, locked jaws
advancing, always advancing
into and over your helpless frame methodically

Such purpose
and beauty
in its decomposing decadence

Reality is Socially-Sanctioned Fantasy

the ghosts and Titans of the mind
are formulated
and sculpted from fragments
or merged synapses;
phantoms, formless and lost,
emerge from the Grey and White
into sun and atmosphere
taking on bronze and stone
we pray were flesh and blood

in places where there are chairs in chairs
and spears in pillars,
captured essences preserved
stagnant, ready, and patient
we make fever-dreams into epics
and glimpses of alternate realms

expecting to transpose them with our own
like wet membranes—organic tissue—we
we bind them with sound minds
we give purpose to the soundless and formless

A Sharp Pill

It is a strange thing to love a place
and feel imbued with an atmosphere
to take nourishment from even the sun
as though you were tall and green
and vibrant in the sway of
the melodic fields of home.

It is stranger still to grow foreign
in that place
and to feel your very hide crawl
with panic in the pallid air
in which you once flourished.

To hate your home is to hate living;
flee swiftly with terror and longing!

Where the Devil Hides

There is a torturous silence
that invades the peace and quiet—
yes, they can be separated, analyzed,
dissected, and labeled as
two distinct creatures—between moments.

You drink coffee, feed birds, and go to bed
between these moments—then they are not
the "in-between moments anymore—and
you live suspended in some liminal,
snow-globe life; the entrance to boredom, no, horror.

Pick up and move, alter your course,
and still you remain in solitude.
we wade in the irritatingly calm waters
of the discreet silences and wait.
Satan exists here.

Rock Bottom

Your absence interrupts our progress
days pass, and nights, and
I am still screaming at ruined egg yolks
dripping into the albumen of disappointment
and false expectations
throwing shovels at cars feels good, I swear
although my thoughts are erratic,
my actions feign constancy
for the sake of masculinity,
pretend you have no desire
threatening females and power struggles
pull at in-grown hairs of insecurities
nothing is more painful than words unspoken,
taboos unbroken, and images
you could have prevented,
haunting you in the solitude of your regret.

The Uncertain Beast

Uncertainty bears down
and cracks us at our seams
where interior regions lock tight
like porcelain banks, split
and robbed of all intrinsic value
there is nothing to invest in a mind
riddled with anticipation
the anxiety-ridden mind froths
monotonously and with singular purpose
like drowning waves buckling and pounding
there is no mercy in the sparks of
a hammer on an anvil either

We maim and tether this demon
with precision and accuracy,
timing and sureties, but
they are only platitudes
pray and beg, weep and suffer,

we are self-contained executioners of
our own crippled sense of entitlement
slaughtering expectation is like
skinning a still-breathing cobra
its scaled shaft glistening of predation
and spitting, spitting
as you, violet and floating,
slip away.

Pyrrhic Victories

I always recall that
Pride goeth before Destruction; He leads Her
yet can never hold my tongue
or melt my heart one moment
before I am vindicated and made to
feel understood

Headstrong women vow
subconsciously to break all men
continued defiance of an abandoned patriarchy
it's no wonder we have always
attempted subjugation and
reined them in to save ourselves!

Insecurity is the monotonous and
clichéd enemy equipped with lives for
constant resurrection
we will never pass through this
narrow passage of dulled confidence
like this

We are all men, all women
to each other
we rail against powerlessness
and war for a victory that has already
been gained in each others' arms
in this abode of emotive expression

There is no difference in our woeful battles
against each other just as
there is no difference in each other
just as there is no difference between
the blood in our veins and the
red leaves falling now

The End Result of a Failed Marriage that Began with Such Burning Love

We will end up
>hating each other
>longing for each other
>knowing we cannot live
>>with each other
>but knowing we cannot
>kill the urges or ourselves
>at a distance
>>until the day we die.

Ancient Struggle

Two red of the reddest red birds
stretched their brilliant, feathered, crimson
wings like muscled arms bleeding from
mud-drenched battle
and jetted to the damp just-after-May-shower
grass to enact the ancient struggle of
scripted competition.

A pile of cerise now, their threats
and ruddy countenances echoing
the cries of successful genetic forebears
who granted them such gleaming iridescence
and thirsty, violent demeanors:
blood for blood, wing-tip for wing-tip
in a war of vermillion.

They meet and scourge,
screech and wail in
muted bird-tongue bent on the
merciless pursuit of brown-breasted
lackluster counterparts
for momentary copulation
just as momentary and anti-climactic,
they end the performance and flee the stage
from the cardinal masculine sacrifice.

Roaring Chickens

I rode in a truck today with a chicken on my lap
I tied the roosters' muck-covered feet
scaled remnants of a reptilian past
He could have been a king of them
with bailer twine just right
the shining yellow and gold flaking armor snowed
on my legs as he lay silently on his back- defeated
for a short time

Some mariachi eased the trip and tied it all together:
Bright sun, clear sky, summer day
creeping, funerary truck bouncing
with the nonchalance accompanying
the creation of a childhood memory

I laugh at the behavior of roosters
their cunning is conspicuous and shadows our own
they are flurries of wings and screams

Mating involves: discovering bits
of phantom food, a short dance,
and brutal rape
Fighting involves: bullied shoves and side-stares,
overdramatized combat, and bloody deaths for
Unprepared Submissives

There is a line between dancing and fighting for a cock
like young boys with their fathers' guns
threatening with hormones
until bullets claim lives

We roar like chickens
conspicuous and headstrong,
daring and battle-thirsty,
fighting until the last step
to the table of slaughter

Country Settlements

Wind-dried gray bird boxes dot
fence posts in abandoned, fallow fields
soaked with heavy morning dampness after a heavy
night downpour
thick mists rise on black-tree horizons
in the silence of fogged gravel roads
where no one speaks

There's nothing I want to hear
there's nothing I want to know
there's no learning to be had in these
desolate stagnant ponds of the interior
some stillness is a prison
the water in the mind breaks and ripples

Dissatisfaction rises from muddy depths
and dissipates into the clouded atmosphere
charged with the energy of an All Soul's
the membrane between the Nothing that grows
and the clamoring for hopeful revelry
in a stupor of optimism thickens into a blockade

Idols fall and all around us,
companions fade into the murk of memory
like lines of soldiers before the firing squads
we pretend that every bit of airborne lint
glowing with reflected sunlight floating before us
is a sign and proof—we smile and sign heavily
Tired of the fight, we sink
into still waters, silent roads, and fogged earth
there is virtue in domesticity
but the coward often lives
while the brave sprints first
into the burning fires of senseless abandon

Social Logic

I saved my grandfathers' last pouch of
Chewing tobacco
Its spiced stink, its earthy dampness
Still pressed tight in a roll
Like it was when it lived in his back pocket

It's a contagion piece that touched him
So it's a piece of him
So I keep it to be with him
We've always lived in our heads
Human nature only touches nature
It doesn't reside there.

Blood of the World

There are times when,
sitting in silence with a blank
Mind,
admiring painted walls, pink and
orange lights streaming through
brown trees like wind,
that you can feel
the Blood of the World move in you
and know that you are a piece
of the lived-experience of consciousness;
you are content.